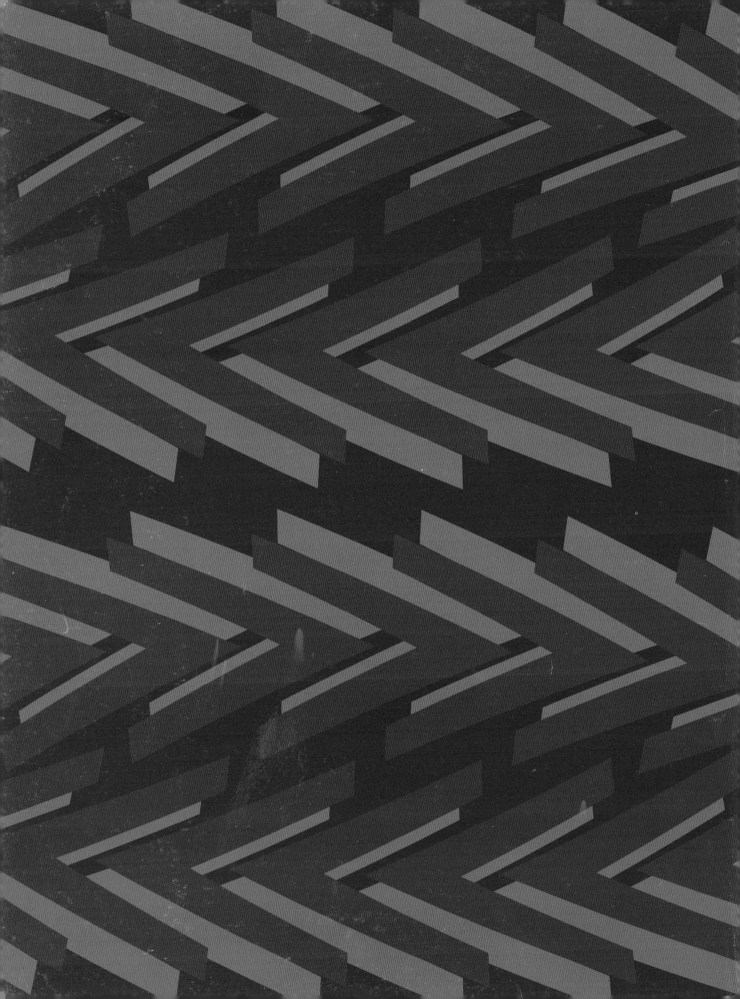

This is my racing car

Written by Chris Oxlade
Photography by Andy Crawford

FRANKLIN WATTS
LONDON • SYDNEY

This edition 2009

Franklin Watts
338 Euston Road
London NW1 3BH

Franklin Watts Australia
Hachette Children's Books
Level 17/207 Kent Street
Sydney NSW 2000

Editor: Jennifer Schofield
Designer: Jemima Lumley
Photography: Andy Crawford
Racing car driver: Rodolfo Gonzalez

Acknowledgements:
Jakob Ebrey: p21; p23; p24; p25; p27
The Publisher would like to thank Russell Eacott, Rodolfo Gonzalez,
Olly Smith and all at T-Sport for their help in producing this book.
Every attempt has been made to clear copyright.
Should there be any inadvertent omission please
apply to the publisher for rectification.

A CIP catalogue record for this book
is available from the British Library.

ISBN: 978 0 7496 8915 5
Dewey Classification: 629'228

Printed in China

Franklin Watts is a division of Hachette Children's Books,
an Hachette Livre UK company.
www.hachettelivre.co.uk

Contents

> Me and my racing car

Hello! This mega machine is a racing car. I am a racing car driver.

*I drive my car in races.
My car is very, very fast.*

▷ Racing car power

My racing car is pushed
along by an engine.

⌃ *The engine is under
the engine cover.*

▷ *To see the engine,
the mechanic takes
off the engine cover.*

> The engine
needs fuel to
make it work.
The fuel goes
in here.

> Wheels and tyres

The engine makes the back wheels go round. The wheels push the car along the track.

▲ *The tyres are wide. They stop the car sliding about on the race track.*

◁ *This tyre is for dry weather.*

▽ *This tyre is for rainy weather. The grooves help the tyre to grip the track.*

▽ *The mechanic has taken off the tyre to check the brakes. I use the brakes to slow the car down.*

brake

▷ The bodywork

My car is covered with smooth bodywork. It lets the car go quickly.

The mechanic lifts off some of the bodywork to fix the parts underneath.

This piece of bodywork is called the nose cone.

3

▶ The wings

The wings press the car down as it zooms along. This helps the tyres to grip the track.

> *The rear wing presses the back tyres down.*

∨ *The front wing presses the front tyres down.*

▷ The cockpit

I sit in the cockpit. It is full
of controls for driving the car.

△ *I press buttons on the steering wheel
when I want to go faster or slower.*

I take the steering wheel off to get in and out of the cockpit.

▷ Ready to drive

I wear special clothes when I drive my car. They keep me safe if I have an accident.

▷ *My racing suit, gloves and shoes are all fireproof.*

◁ *My helmet protects my head. Inside are headphones for the team radio.*

The mechanic does up my harness and puts on my steering wheel. I am ready to drive!

> Testing and practice

I am part of a big team
that races the car.

▲ *When I test drive the car,*
I tell the mechanics if there
are things that need to be fixed.

▽ *In the days before a race,
I practise driving round the track.*

▶ At the race

Today is race day!

▲ *My car is taken to the race track in a big truck.*

 I have to drive really quickly to overtake the other cars.

The race is over when the black-and-white flag is waved.

> More racing cars

Here are some more racing cars that I drive.

▲ *This is a kart. My first racing car was a kart.*

This is a touring car. It is like the cars you see on the road, but it goes much faster!

Be a racing car driver

It takes a lot of hard work to become a racing car driver.

You have to learn about the different parts of the car.

You have to practise driving the car for hours and hours to learn to drive fast and safely.

Racing car parts

helmet

rear wing

cockpit

wheel

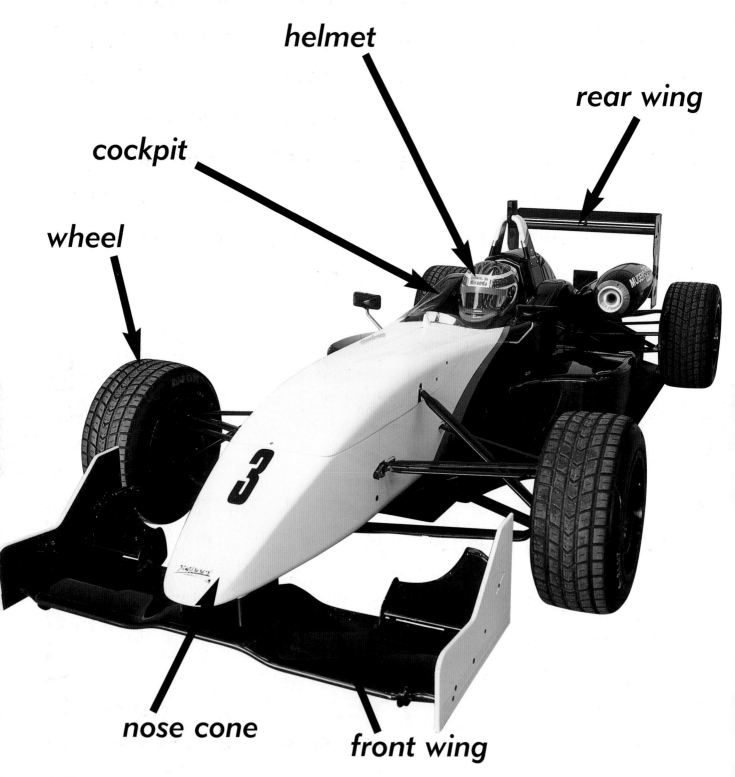

nose cone

front wing

> Word bank

body work – the metal part of the car that covers things such as the engine

cockpit – where the driver sits

engine – the part of a racing car that makes it move

fireproof – something that will not catch fire

harness – the strap that keeps drivers in the cockpit

mechanic – the person who fixes the racing car

team radio – the special radio that lets a driver talk to his team while he is racing

rear – back

Websites

This racing car is from the T-Sport Formula 3 team. To find out more about the car and the driver, Rodolfo Gonzalez, log on to www.t-sportgroup.com

Index